YOUR KNOWLEDGE HAS VALUE

AF667068

- We will publish your bachelor's and master's thesis, essays and papers
- Your own eBook and book - sold worldwide in all relevant shops
- Earn money with each sale

Upload your text at www.GRIN.com and publish for free

GRIN

Mumtaz Mazumdar

A review of the novel "The Inheritance of Loss" by Kiran Desai

GRIN Publishing

Bibliographic information published by the German National Library:

The German National Library lists this publication in the National Bibliography; detailed bibliographic data are available on the Internet at http://dnb.dnb.de .

This book is copyright material and must not be copied, reproduced, transferred, distributed, leased, licensed or publicly performed or used in any way except as specifically permitted in writing by the publishers, as allowed under the terms and conditions under which it was purchased or as strictly permitted by applicable copyright law. Any unauthorized distribution or use of this text may be a direct infringement of the author s and publisher s rights and those responsible may be liable in law accordingly.

Imprint:

Copyright © 2011 GRIN Verlag, Open Publishing GmbH
Print and binding: Books on Demand GmbH, Norderstedt Germany
ISBN: 978-3-656-36641-6

This book at GRIN:

http://www.grin.com/en/e-book/176709/a-review-of-the-novel-the-inheritance-of-loss-by-kiran-desai

GRIN - Your knowledge has value

Since its foundation in 1998, GRIN has specialized in publishing academic texts by students, college teachers and other academics as e-book and printed book. The website www.grin.com is an ideal platform for presenting term papers, final papers, scientific essays, dissertations and specialist books.

Visit us on the internet:

http://www.grin.com/

http://www.facebook.com/grincom

http://www.twitter.com/grin_com

A review of the novel *"The Inheritance of Loss"* by Kiran Desai

Kiran Desai wrote the novel *The Inheritance of Loss* and it is conferred the Man Booker prize in 2006, National Critics Circle Fiction Award in 2007 and the 2006 Vodafone Crossword Book Award. Desai is the youngest female to win the Booker prize.

Kiran Desai was born in New Delhi in 3rd January 1971. At 14 years of age, she and her mother moved to England. In one year, they moved to USA. Her first novel is *Hullaballo in the Guava Orchard.* Desai is woman. It is generally expected that any female writer can portray only the female psyche and characters, as protagonists. Desai proves it as narrow prediction. In this novel, she is dexterously able to portray male psyche. She is daughter of prominent writer Anita Desai, who was thrice shortlisted for Booker Prize. Her daughter won it for *The Inheritance of Loss*. This is Kiran Desai's second novel.

The loci are Kalimpong and New York. The two worlds of these two places are totally different. A mundane reality of the two places is rather visible. Undoubtedly, the marginalized human beings of both the places are shown in the novel. It is to be noted that New York is a renowned place in earth. Whereas, Kalimpong was rather unknown until Desai took notice of it. Kalimpong is micro setting in comparison to New York. And Desai could relate the two places finely as nothing lesser than one part of the earth with one kind of human beings. Desai realized that one's place in earth is merely incidental. It is matter of perspective too. The location cannot be firm at all. The past, present and future too are part of the location.

The protagonists of the story are the retired judge, his grand-daughter Sai, their cook, and Biju, the son of the cook. There are peripheral characters that too help in the development of various themes through their different tales. The novel opens with Sai, her anglophile grandfather, the cook and the dog Mutt. Gyan is the lover of Sai. Biju, Lola, Noni, SaeedSaeed, and Harish-Harry are other important characters. These characters are spread between New York and Kalimpong.

The characters stand against their personal spheres with larger issues of political turmoil, racialism, immigrant experiences, and regionalism. Kiran Desai clams all these experiences of the characters in one story. They are in their own journeys. The personal identity of each character is revealed. Yet these are related to global issues. Almost all the characters have encounters with the West. Gyan, who confesses that he was only human and so sometimes weak, echoes the other characters too. The anglophile Judge had only turned into self-hatred. When Sai saw Gyan in the rebellion, she walked home slowly. Situations like this foiled the personal hopes of love and affairs. The revolution was threatening the personal joys of Sai, a minor girl. The cook tried to remind Sai that the capabilities of Gyan were not bright. Sai is affected by Gyan, who gets involved in the ethnic, Nepali revolution. It is observed often that love takes place amidst unequal partners. The result of this love also is unequal. Their bash-up adds to her loneliness too. The extremist rebellion has dented their kinship and spurted out the repressed differences. Both Sai and Gyan suddenly start becoming aware of the class of each other. The turmoil of the public agitation seems to unearth many truths about the characters. The revolution acts symbolic here.

The dormant feelings gets vent with the help of this symbolic revolution. The revolution made the judge, Jemubhai vulnerable, due to his hunting rifles. The Gorkhaland agitation creeps in the lives of the characters. The judge when away from chess would look like a mask put on his face. Suddenly, he would remember his personality and go back to his chess. The desire of the Gorkhaland has led to a revolution. They wanted a homeland where they would not be treated as servants. Young boys in this attempt to become men, looted houses and collected ammunition. There turns out to be so much of chaos that the natives there think of not flushing for saving water. Neighbour turns against neighbour. There was absence of gas and kerosene. Biju, in America was facing the parallel universe of displacement and stumbling from one job to another. The negative aspects of living as an illegal alien in New York are seen. The universe was not in the business of justice. To all these, even the sun was hot and cast no shadow. This casting of no shadow by the Sun, reminds of noon-time, metaphoric of the crisis at its zenith.

The judge, who always identified himself with the British, stands in the width of shade of the knife. The shadows of the nights chomped as if, like his memories of past. This man, Jemubhai, who dressed for dinner, even in the jungle, later, remains without socks all the time. The physical identities seemed to have gone crossed too along with the inner recesses. He has just one friend in his world, Bose. His constant lonely companionship with chess without a dual player reminds and signifies the white British Empire, which ruled many parts of the world without a competitor at par. It was almost a one-sided kingship and domination. This kind of representation coincides with any contemporary age, where there might be just one or a few leaders to follow. The embittered, reptilian judge is lost in the symbolic chessboard and in his memories of humiliation in a foreign land. The life of the judge is so lonely that only a pet dog can fit in his solitude. This also echoes the common cliché that one who thinks and behaves as superior is likely to be left alone. He had no cementing relation in the past with his illiterate wife. Now, in the present, he can build no relation with granddaughter, Sai, although, they lived under the same roof. The signs and themes of loss, loneliness and racialism-impacts are seen in the life of the judge. He is disgusted with human beings, after bitter racial experiences during the Cambridge days. Actually, we are all historically situated despite it is of contemporary events.

Biju is another victim of loneliness and loss, in the dual Indian-American upbringing. Almost all characters are lonely and unfulfilled from each other, in the nation or outside it. Biju is an illegal migrant, who went to America as cheap labourer. The life of Biju can be compared and contrasted with his father. Both remain labourers. It is ironical that the cook is nationless inside the nation. His son, Biju, is nationless outside. Both are suffering from their own sense of loss, truth, untruths, and loneliness. The American Dream is inadequate to fulfill the emotional and basic needs of Biju. It goes ironical with the Judge who is ashamed and dislikes his heritage, culture and even the colour of his skin. He fuels the sense of rejection in his soul in his whole life. The clashes of races, classes, cultures, generations, are filtered through the characters.

There is a concurrent telling of the story of two different kinds of Diasporas - that of undocumented and thereby exploited blue-collar immigrants in New York and an ageing, elitist cluster of Indian professionals settled post retirement in a remote Gurkha hill station. Both Diasporas face challenges of a normally globalized society that is paradoxically fraught with increasingly exclusivist, separatist, and nationalistic agendas. Diaspora collapses the boundaries between the first world and the third world while simultaneously enforcing them. Earlier, Britain could not hem the gaps as the colonizer of commonwealth nations. Today, the United States has failed too and the apparel only tatters further.

This text of Kiran Desai reveals new subjects and new knowledge about the people of two places located in entirely two different parts of the world. The India that Desai knew in childhood was then a closed door economic policy country. The world arrived only through books and they meant everything. Despite diasporic, to Desai, this book The Inheritance of Loss is like a return journey to the fact of being Indian. New York gave half the narrative. For rest half, she has to take help of India.

The book deals with the implicit reference to past British colonialism. Jemubhai is filled with humiliation because of being Indian. The text can be approached with eye to history. The value of history can be rediscovered. This text is influenced by historical reality.

We inherit loss from past. Like ants men would make their paths and civilization and their wars once again only to be washed once again. Sai lost her parents. The involvement of Gyan in the revolution was uprooted. The revolution was only a vent passage to his pent-up rage and frustrations. And it becomes a loss to Sai too. The east-west meet is the inheritance and the losses derived from it too are the inheritance. It was an irony that United States, a country built on the finest principles could give only losses to an immigrant like Biju. It is a paradox that the question of homeland was same as in the land of the three Ts land of tea, timber, and tourism as it is in America. And this was the America which is in the process of buying the world. Again, it was stunning that, Biju was jealous of his own son. And, jealousy was a third world chip on the shoulder. Sai, the Judge, and Biju are all dual-nation related.

The book has invited diverse interpretations, as being dissolved in rich, eloquent prose, aided by the fictional characters, with themes like, the sense of loss, contemporary global issues of multiculturalism, economic inequality, fundamentalism, terrorism, postcolonial chaos, challenge of assimilation, comic joy, nationhood, conflicting desires, modernity, increasingly interconnected world, realism, identity-crisis, love and hate, past and present, dislocation, tragedies of the freed third world countries, exile, American dream, power hierarchy, homecoming, loneliness, truth, untruth, cultural identity, class-system, ethnicity, and racism.

These themes are sub-genred with some micro themes, doughed with the aforementioned macro themes. They may be slotted as, the Nepali struggle to enter the mainstream subcontinent, the unequal love-affair between Sai and Gyan; Indian ire with past colonialism, the dilemmas and despair exploded after colonial suppression; the theme of the intersection of East-West and the changes both the two parts undergo and display inadequate progress. The pain of exile is illuminated; there are the themes of depth, emotion, hilarity, insight and imagination. National and racial identity is portrayed too.

The theme of loss and sadness is a major theme. The Indian class system alienates the citizens further, from the clam of nationhood and so on. The loss of faith in India leads the citizens to become immigrants. The personal anecdotes of the characters twine against the wider social, economic, and political backdrops of the two places. The personal becomes the political and vice versa. The novel's historical setting of the novel is considered to be the 1980s. But, colonial era of India is invoked too. However, we see post 9/11 elements in this personal and globally exploded-themed novel.

Love which is an important theme of the novel recurs in the novel. Noni never had love in her life. To Lola, the servants experienced love from the economic structure of relationship. The judge is always filled with detest. To the cook, the greatest love is love that is never shown. To him, love is looking after someone, and someone looking after you. Money was not everything in life and love. Years ago, as a student of oxford, Uncle Potty had considered himself a lover of love. During his practical research trips, he had found pure love in the most sordid of spots, the wrong sides of town where the police did not venture. Some loved him while he did not love them; others he loved madly, deeply, and they, did not love him at all. Some loved him while he did not love them; others he loved madly, deeply, and they, did not love him at all. Again, in these different forms of love, Sai had her own experience towards life around her. Since her romance with Gyan, Sai had a new understanding with cats. It is stunning that her love-affair only changes her attitude towards cats only. Again, these cats remind of some repressed or hidden physical desires in Sai. It reminds of "The love-song of J. Alfred Prufrock," written by T. S. Eliot where the lazy cat echoes the hidden desires of Prufrock. Also, after Gyan gets involved in the rebellion, Sai stands before the mirror and thinks upon how in the fight for a new homeland, Gyan has forgotten her. And she was already in a family, which never cared of her. The judge almost wept at the loss of Mutt. To him, a man was not equal to animal. Human life was stinking and corrupt. These were the beautiful creatures that lived with so much delicacy and did no harm to others. He dreamt that Mutt was dying but was hardly aware of his only kin, Sai at home. It was a sad thing that, schools and hospitals only meant civilization. Never again would the father of judge know that love for a human being was not adulterated by another. Gyan prefers to death than remain slaved, poster-like and stateless. Mutt, the dog was taken for a winter coat. It was an irony that when all was life and death for the natives there, when the animal got lost, the judge and Sai seemed to have to do nothing else left in their lonely, lost lives, except searching Mutt. The image of broken umbrellas hanging oddly like injured birds, represent the physical and mental condition of the people around them.

Time plays another important theme in the structure of the narrative of the novel. It is seen that, condensation fogged the glasses of the clock of Cho Oyu. That is, the people in that house could not see the importance of the present time. The contemporariness is blurred. Noni, the anglophile neighbour advises Sai, never to go by life, where time does not pass. "Time should move." But, we see that the beings of Cho Oyu are living lives contradictory to these statements. Language plays an important role in the expression of the characters. Sai became confused in a capillary web of paths. In this image of web, a giant tiger-stripped spider sits. Did language gave relief in all these chaos, or it was the language which eulogized all the thoughts and chaos in physical forms around them? Even the words coming out of the mouths of the characters seem like shadows. Comedy plays important role in the structure. The rooster crows like the colonial. Hunger skips like the little mouse, also coincides with the Hindi phrase in India, of rats running in the tummy due to hunger. A tooth could be found in the bloodshed areas, is comic and at the same time speaks of violence. Memory plays another important role in relation to past and present. Memories are said to be like "diamonds." To Biju, coming among the English was like coming back to snatch the bread which their fathers had snatched from the colonized. Biju found himself smiling at the memory of the time when the whole village had watched India win a test match against Australia on a television which was running of a car battery because the transformer in the village had burnt. To Biju, a memory was more beautiful than real things in life around him. A common memory was an establishment of truth. As the cook recalled the stories, they seemed more and more true. The revisitation of the Judge to the past, is also related to his bitter memories to past. The trunks are symbolic and “jog” his past memory. The shadows of the nights chomped as if, are his memories. Memory is an implicit theme too.

Migration and living between two worlds and between past and present are the other themes. Truthful revelation of the workings of thoughts of the characters is another important theme.

The story and structure of the novel help in building the themes. The recurring images play the most important roles in knotting the themes and form a unity. The image of the “mist” is dominant and ties too, the structure of the narrative. In Kanchenjunga, it is compared to “a moving creature”. It has been given human attributes. It is compared to the “caress” in the hairs of Sai. It gets live comparison when compared to a dragon. The functioning mist blurs the thieves. It is like a runaway when “cows boom through the mist.” These images remind of Charles Dickens landmark novel, “Great Expectations.” The smoke and the mist in his novel guide the state of the blurred characters in industrial England. Vapor, shadow and fog also play similar patterns in this novel of Desai. Shadow plays important role when, “the trees turned into silhouettes.” The scorpion is said to have a silhouette like a human being. The animals and insects get human attributes. The novelist transfers or exchanges the qualities as, unavailability of aright and necessary attributes to the human and non-human beings. “The solitude of the past-obsessed judge, became a habit, the habit became the man, and it crushed him into a shadow. But shadows, after all, create their own unease, and despite his attempts to hide, he merely emphasized something that unsettled others.” “The mist under the dial might lift a sad state for the civilized man.” The dial reminds of time and history around the characters. The role of the “settling mist of evening” gets over as it “swept down” but Mutt the lost dog did not appear. In Desai’s turmoiled world, the blurry mist catches the speed of the more unclear smoke. Once, we see that the thickening mist adds to “the dusk and the vapor.” The mist and the vapor seem to direct the narrative of the novel. There is “a several legged banyan tree in its pillared shade.” The writer seems to be at a loss in deciphering the correct attribute Even the words coming out of the mouths of the characters seem like shadows. Vapor is compared to “ribbony curls.”

The insignificant, yet powerful “powdery mist can burn off the sun.” This mist is so powerful, that the Sun is hardly mentioned. The mist echoes the human conditions around it. Again, there is the dependent "tender mist under the watery sun." It is stunning to see that the Sun is called watery. Other images are like; snow of Kanchenjunga is compared to "plume." The "bald lightbulb" is said to be dangling. Bulb is said to be "bald" like the human beings. The bulb begins to "buzz like the beetle," when near the judge. Scorpions are compared to a "community." Soot is called "thickets" and "batlike." The squid's eyes are compared to "as big as apples." The squid was considered to be last of its kind. It was becoming something like the dodo. The decrepit house Cho Oyu is compared to "a thousand deceased spiders lay scattered like dead blossoms on the attic floor." The structure of the judge is of the same "house seemed fragile in the balance of this night-just a husk." Walls swelled like sails, they were flailing. The judge who barely felt human at all, is also said to be surrounded by "shadowy halls" in his house. A house is supposed to cast Sun-shadow outside itself. But, the house of Jemubhai casts within it. This refers to the oppressed psychology unrecognized mental agony of the beings living inside the house, where there is no presence of light. Cho Oyu was full of shadow. By the end of his life, the "untidy" "mongrel" judge preferred "shadow" to light, and faded days to sunny, for he was suspicious that sunlight might reveal him, and his hideousness, all too clearly.

The other images are the big rocks along thin paths that veined the mountains. Poetic language use aids Desai to weave the messages much better. To Gyan, the sky seemed, "spidery stars through the prehistoric ferns." The telephones have rictus. And the frogs seem to have swallowed their dial-tones. Again, kissing Gyan by Sai seems like morphing him like a frog. Even kiss, an intimate expressive symbol of love and attachment goes awry here and it stunningly morphs lover to a traditionally, upraised, ugly animal like frog. As Biju approaches the Gandhi café, the air suddenly becomes solid. Beings were compared to big bacterial clumps. Here, humans being compared to bacteria reminds of the inevitable, insignificant multiplicity. And very rare bacteria are of usefulness. When the thieves arrived in Cho Oyu, trees were hung with limbs of enemies. The nature had already started taking the form of unnaturalness and absurdity. Other images are like; snow of Kanchenjunga is compared to "plume." The "bald lightbulb" is said to be dangling. The bulb begins to "buzz like the beetle," when near the judge. It is surprising that, the poisonous scorpions move in "community" but not human beings. Soot is called "thickets" and "batlike." The squid's eyes are compared to "as big as apples." Biju dreams that he will have so many grandchildren that they will "swat like flies." Alas, we can think of our future generations in comparison to insignificant insects like flies only. Kanchenjunga is compared to "collared by a cloud." This collar image speaks of the still sturdy mountains. Snakes lay "roasting" in the mountainside.

Dark and light play as contrasting elements in connection to the characters of this novel of Desai. Against this black and white background of the chessboard, there take place many other issues of the lives of the characters, philosophical and historical. Sai is compared to an orphaned child of the romance between India and the soviets. The stubbornly, dumb mirror reminds her of the changeable physical beauty. Before the mirror, her heart was lying in pieces. She later on stops seeing herself in it anymore. Once, Jemubhai, compares himself to "invisible self", when his "phantom" mother, was pouring cold water in the "dark" courtyard.

The black and white chessboard of Jemubhai remains the center of his thought and life in later life. The faces have cabbage-leaved "shadows" shape. The "shadows" of leaves recur in the novel. The cook who was in search of his son, Biju, leaped at every "shadow" for him. "Deadly nightshade was blooming" occur a line in the novel. A rat moves towards the "shadow." The image and symbol of shadow vehicles to reveal the ins and outs of the characters. Apart from the mist, and shadow other objects of Nature of Kalimpong play an important role in echoing the inner thoughts of the characters. The heat always reminded the snobbish Judge of his nationality. The "flying squirrels" chased each other through the circination of ferns and mist. The winter has a sterile smell.

There are post-colonial elements present in the novel. Here, the prefix post may be said to imply a chronological sequence and the aftermath of colonialism. Not just Biju may be related being as, the post-colonial Indian, but also that what takes place in Kalimpong too. Both the situations address the international audience of English speakers. The novel also refers to centuries of economic and cultural power of the subjugation of the West.

There is a structural unity in the novel. The novel starts with the description of the five peaks and ends with the five peaks. There is chaos in the novel, from the theft in Cho Oyu to the revolution. Kalimpong had become a ghost town from beauty and plume. But, again the five peaks of Kalimpong turned golden. And that seemed the apparent truth. But, at last it ends towards silence and routine.

There is hope and optimism by the end of the novel. Father Booty tells Sai, to always look at the horizon that always helps. Congress of hopeful frogs continued to sing. May be, like many entire nations, Gorkhaland would also appear overnight and give relief to the desires of the natives of that place. The damp wood was not giving right fire, when lit by the cook in the beginning of the narrative. In the end, the soggy match was tried to be lit by Sai and at last, it lit and flared. Fire also may be said to mean life and civilization. The beginning of the novel and the end with it shows an aright structure put up by the writer. The juxtaposition of qualities in the images and the symbols also speak volumes of the ability of poetic conversions in the famous novel by Kiran Desai.